Rigging the Wind

*To Herman + Micheline,
with love —*

Rigging the Wind

Jennifer Barber

JENNIFER BARBER

KORE PRESS TUCSON 2003

Rigging the Wind is the winner of the Kore Press First Book Award for 2002, selected by Jane Miller.

Coyright©2003 Kore Press
all rights reserved
ISBN 1-888553-15-4

Kore Press, Inc
PO Box 3044
Tucson, AZ 85702-3044
www.korepress.org

TO MY PARENTS AND FOR PETE

ACKNOWLEDGMENTS

Agni, "Vendaval"

Fulcrum, "Pines," "Drifting" (as "Canción"), "Fourth Room of the Exhibition," "Travels in Place"

Harvard Review, "Reinante," "Opening a Jewish Encyclopedia"

Heliotrope, "Notes"

Journal of Modern Writing, "A Judeo-converso, ca. 1470"

Judaism, "After the Night Train," "1497"

Marlboro Review, "This Morning"

96 Inc., "Summer in the Attic"

Orion, "Vaseful of Wild Roses"

Partisan Review, "These"

Poetry, "Summer as a Large, Reclining Nude"

Poems and Plays, "Leaving" (originally published as "Days of 1492")

Salamander, "Conspiracy of Silence," "Word," "Self-Portrait," "Song" (co-translated from the Punjabi by Irfan Malik and Jennifer Barber)

Four Way Reader #2 (Four Way Books, 2001): "Summer in the Attic," "Nights," "A Village I Love," "Photograph of My Mother, a Girl in Central Park"

Take Three: 3, Agni New Poets Series (Graywolf Press, *1998*): "Vaseful of Wild Roses," "A Village I Love," "Nights," "Photograph of My Mother, a Girl in Central Park," "Vendaval," "Six Brightnesses,"

"Table," "Summer as a Large, Reclining Nude," "San Miguel," "Blue Dress"

I am grateful to Lisa Bowden of Kore Press and Jane Miller, judge of the 2002 contest. I wish to thank Pam Bernard, Irfan Malik, Fred Marchant, Susan Monsky, and Jacquelyn Pope for their early readings of this collection.

Contents

Introduction by Jane Miller 11

I
Conspiracy of Silence 15
Summer in the Attic, I'm Taking Off My Skirt 16
Vaseful of Wild Roses 17
Hymns in the Wind 18

II
from *The Word* 25
San Miguel 26
A Village I Love 27
Reinante 29
Nights 30
Storm at Sun Up 32
After the Night Train 34
Vendaval 35

III
Self-Portrait 36
Opening a Jewish Encyclopedia 37
Photograph of My Mother, a Girl in Central Park 38
These 39
Nightfall 40
A *Judeo-converso,* ca. 1470 42
Leaving 46
1497 48
Gate 50

IV
Song 51
Six Brightnesses 52
In the House of a Friend of a Friend 58
This Morning 59
Reading in Bed at the Inn 61
Fourth Room of the Exhibition 62
Longing in Passover Week 63
Summer as a Large, Reclining Nude 65
Drifting 66
Pines 68
Travels in Place 69
Reading Borges While the Baby Naps 71
Blue Dress 72
Table 74
The Adoption 75
Judía 76
Notes 77

Notes 78

Introduction by Jane Miller

> *I lit the kindling:*
> *a forest in the grate*
> *woke inside*
> *an orange city*

In brief, refreshing lines, Jennifer Barber presents familial scenes and spiritual epiphanies at a time when the world needs poetry desperately and needs that poetry to be about essences. Using the wind as her chief metaphor, she works with a painter's affection for color and image to create, with a few brush strokes, landscapes haunted by human suffering. We instantly recognize her world; it is ours. Quiet alarms sound.

> *In the ports,*
> *the boats are being filled*
>
> *with rabbis and translators,*
> *shopkeepers and wool merchants.*
>   (from "Leaving")

In subjects ranging from the expulsion of the Jews in the fifteenth century to intimacies between contemporary lovers, we are made to feel our own needs and terrors expressed, our own cities left behind. These poems are transparent, yet everywhere reflect things and people darkly, in emergency. And yet — or, also — how intimately the world is perceived:

*Spain, I have more names
than a cherry tree has leaves.*

*Let me sleep with you tonight
half a world away,*

*forgetting the sad centuries.
Just you and me, and the warm spring night.*

The world is revered, the world is mourned, and the world is renewed, in the tradition of the most beautiful Mediterranean lyrics. A perusal of the poem titles will give the first sense of the accurate, clean expression to come. The poems themselves provide sharp images and metaphors to experience: there are rivers and farms, there are oranges hardened on a branch, and one's attention is caught up in them while, and after, reading these poems. I have been startled by Jennifer Barber's swift, deft touch. Language once again has become "yours alone":

*I've imagined you
standing in the square*

*of an old city.
The shops are closed.*

*No bustle, no cars.
Language,*

yours alone,
drifts on the still air.

Welcome to *Rigging the Wind,* something you have now found, and may you enjoy it.

Jane Miller
TUCSON, ARIZONA
FEBRUARY 26, 2003

I

Conspiracy of Silence

Amrita Pritam

Night is dozing
someone has broken
into a human ribcage:
the theft is of our dreams

the footprints of the thieves
are scattered on city streets
and every country's roads

no eye sees their trace
or becomes alarmed

only sometimes, someone's
poem, like a chained dog, barks

Summer in the Attic, I'm Taking Off My Skirt

It's all right, the neighbors can't see in
though I can hear
their wailing baby.

The air up here
scratches like a Hudson's Bay
blanket by mid-morning.
I drop my shirt

next to the desk,
then my bra, a fancy thing.
Outside, finches work the tree,

pulling invisible
banners of blue sky.
I'm in the catbird seat
with my naked skin

and heart's tongue,
alone. The shrill
monotone of insects tightens like a wire.

Vaseful of Wild Roses

A long bud lets a petal fall—
an early sacrifice.
The eye, a vase,
can't keep the flowers whole.

The shape we know as rose
is their undoing: they
pass through without stopping for
the word to form. They lean

toward us and away, as if
we were the reason
they let go.

Hymns in the Wind

in mem. A. F.

I

All day the rain
wanted to fall.

All night, all fall
I wanted a name
for what I was
without.

Now I know
night enters me,

its sadness
a sailing ship
in the light
beneath each star.

2

A candle, a match,
the window going blind.

Snails on the cabbages
wait for the rain

sowing only itself,
drowning the magpies' cries,

black and white
wings through a tree.

3

I've imagined you
standing in the square

of an old city.
The shops are closed.

No bustle, no cars.
Language,

yours alone,
drifts on the still air.

4

Dust lifts
through my room,
      touching down
too lightly to be swept.

A flock of birds
      swerves above
the shed,

a sudden whole
in the confusion of its pieces.

5

I lit the kindling:
a forest in the grate
woke inside
an orange city.

Can you hear
this place
in a place
I made for you?

6

Stray bees, returning,
bend the wildflowers.

All night the rigging
of the wind

throws me rope
ladders, and lets go.

7

North of the highway,
empty trees.

The wind I probe
for absences

is only a path
for rain,

the weight of distance
bearing down.

II

from The Word

    Irfan Malik

The path
from
womb to
non-womb
is the
untold
saga of
the wind

untold
because it's everywhere

told
because it's everyone

   vendaval: Spanish for windstorm, wind from the sea

San Miguel

Lying in each other's arms
with too few or too many plans
        for living out the borrowed year

we don't ask what we're doing here,
the first year of our marriage.
        The days are bright, the grass

beyond the washtub gleams
like finely blown strands of glass.
        At night we have no visitors,

no witness but the night, the moon
leaning back against a cloud
        as if she couldn't bear this quiet.

A Village I Love

It's stony enough. It's bitter enough.
A boy with a goad in the field
      keeps an ox and plow in line.

Vines cover the window of a shed
like an eye sealed shut by scars.
      Clothespins click

when the wind takes up
whatever the mind won't touch.
      Widows are widows here, they hang

their tears to dry, they have the time.
Magpies on the garden wall
      chase away the smaller birds,

proving they are needle-eyed
masters of all they see.
      They see sudden shifts of light

followed by gusts of rain.
Wind mutinies against the plow,
      the boy's dirt-caked shoe as he

    takes a rolling step. The rain
      snatches his breath and blurs my eyes,
            watching how the field

    bends in on itself, the boy
    swaying ground and furrow to the grief
          that holds what it sees.

Reinante

Dust of wheat
when there was wheat
and on the hill, smoke—the pines

burning on their own
or set on fire.
Next to the burro, a goat,

next to the axe, a scythe.
In a town this small,
no one forgets.

The sunflowers know
what winter is—
frost on the lemons,

a burnt taste in the air.
You drink slowly
at night, alone.

The weight of the unsaid
unfurls a dark
lily in your heart.

Nights

No one here dreams louder
than the wind, knocking

at the doors
where Franco's men

conscripted farmers' sons
fifty years ago. It blows

over strips of farms
no wider than a pony-run

and rivers made of
diphthongs, like the Eo,

through the greedy
heads of eucalyptus trees,

the bearded, maimed
pines, and villages

whose steeples are crowned
with absurdly large

stork nests set awry.
After a card game in the bar,

the men scrape back their chairs.
They leave in twos and threes.

Children and grandchildren
have moved to

cities farther south.
The men are all that's left,

a knock at the door
and the wind's long memory

of a bloody mountain pass
thigh-deep in mud.

Storm at Sun Up

The garden grows frantic
with the scratch of wings
      abandoning the pear

to vendaval, whose moan
is almost human
      which is why the wives

have sleepless nights
and the children
      wake more than once.

Dozing in his yard,
the rooster takes the storm
      as something against him.

The bleary hens, still dazed,
rattle their alarm
      too late to be of any use.

The sun is up. The wind
is blowing and blowing.
      Hung on the line, a skirt

whirls over the skirts of lettuces,
sensual and sheer, half
> fastened, half undone.

After the Night Train

You slept all day
in the hotel.
I went out alone,

circling the bar-cafés.
In the old quarter,
past the synagogue,

the houses were
conversos—one
prosperous,

one made to kneel,
that one,
skinned by flame.

Vendaval

The brown hen, blown
toward the chopping block
and the red-handled axe.

The sea rubbed bare in spots,
the sky El Greco blue
between the forking clouds.

The only gods are seasonal,
the holding back, the giving in,
the mistimed caress

against, not with, desire.
The wind dies as abruptly
as it started yesterday.

The day's late light
falls on us, unequally—
it makes a new map

of the blue bedspread,
luring disappointment
from our eyes and mouths,

letting us begin again.

III

Self-Portrait

   Amrita Pritam

There was a grief I smoked
in silence, like a cigarette:

only a few poems
came out of the ash I flicked away.

Opening a Jewish Encyclopedia

I couldn't find
the entry I wanted.

The days of the calendar
closed ranks

as though I were
the enemy.

A biblical vine
shifted past its name.

Flowers resembled weeds,
weeds, flowers.

A city revolved
on its platter by the sea,

a village
on the tether of the wind.

Photograph of My Mother, a Girl in Central Park

The squirrel is so thin
it must be the Depression.
There you are, feeding him,
wearing a little fur-trimmed coat.

Mother and Father have
made you take your glasses off.
This is the only point
on which they agree.

Unhappy little girl, you smile,
conscious of the camera
as you reach a hand
toward the squirrel on the bench.

Your other hand is clenched.
Sixty years later
will you knock,
an orphan at my door?

These

These are the Days of Awe,
not marked on my calendar.

Their covenant with gravity
lifts and loosens the leaves,
a last warm breeze.

I lie down in the grass.
Fragments of verse
circle me like dogs.

The house of the dove is empty,
an eagle stuns its prey.

Owls wait
in the broken walls
for a darkness they can hear.

Nightfall

        Soria, 1391

We walk
through the left

doorway in the wall
that marks the entrance

to our streets.
Down the slope,

past the old well
where the stones roll underfoot.

I close my shutters,
lower the straw shade.

    .   .

We've heard
about the sudden

blood in market squares,
the burning roofs

of synagogues.
Nothing has

happened here.
I don't believe it will.

They buy their
cloth from us,

their silver crosses
on fine chains.

.   .

An evening among
others that have

come and gone
shrugs off the day's heat.

The night air
is cold.

Smoke from
a single chimney

changes the taste
of my sleep.

A Judeo-converso, *ca. 1470*

I

Adonai, adóname,
cover me, Oh Lord.

If my neighbors hear
the sound of you in my mouth,

too late to turn me in—
this illness is my last.

My wife and son
will need to pawn

some things from the house
but let them keep

the small book by the bed
that reminds us who we were.

2

I've done what I had to do.
My name has no trace.

Last week I visited
the old cemetery

at the edge of town.
My mother and father are there,

have been a long time.
Some of the gravestones are broken.

The letters look broken too,
strange flags and doorless sheds

trying to replant themselves
in the ear of the heart.

3

I dreamed that I was back
in the house
of my grandfather.

Candles had been lit
and he was
pouring wine.

The fields smelled of dung—
it must have been
early spring.

The wine was
no one's blood.
The neighbor who came to the door

with dirt on his shoes
cleared his throat
and apologized

for asking
to borrow a whetstone
so late in the afternoon.

4

Their gaunt son of God—
I try to see him as though
he were a son of mine,

needing food and clothes.
I see him in the sunflowers
at the end of August,

towering with thirst.

Leaving

A synod of crows, a holy afternoon
on which the beaks dispute
the meaning of
the crests of trees.

The slow eyes of the sunflowers
widen in the field.
In the ports,
the boats are being filled

with rabbis and translators,
shopkeepers and wool merchants.

Some went to Navarre,
some of us to Portugal,
some died of plague
and hunger on stalled ships…

Over and over, gone.
And not gone, like the names
of cities left behind,
Córdoba, Valladolid,

and the way my eyes
resemble certain portraits of that time—
a nobleman, a peddler,
a woman staring in a room.

1497

from the account by R. Abraham Saba

Now Portugal, too.

In Guimarães, the town crier said
all books and phylacteries
must be turned over
at the Lisbon synagogue
on pain of death.

We listened,
I stood trembling.

Before we reached the city, I
buried my manuscripts—
last memories of Spain—
under the roots
of an olive tree.

This morning, a man
they beat with straps
for not letting go
of a book of prayers

was kicked to the ground
and taken. Here
in the courtyard
of the great synagogue
no one knows where we are.

Gate

All talk of Granada
has to be
abandoned here,
with all talk of oranges.

What did the fathers' fathers
say before they left?

Secret honey from the hive,
the sweetness of Kabbalah
stopping their lips.

Light through the fog
is motherless and fatherless.

Blood and bread, silver and dung.
Their shadows thin
and disappear.

Under the stone balconies,
a pigeon and a dove
are the same bird.

IV

Song
           Najam Hussain Syed

If you have to live somewhere,
live among trees.
Without counting,
without straining,
they drink the poison,
turning it to nectar.

If you have to live somehow,
live among trees.
Without asking,
without telling,
they light the green lamps
and place them on our eyes.

Six Brightnesses

I

The grass is dry, the long
end-of-summer wind is here.

A child in the park
squints as he slides

down the slow metal slide.

The air is bright all afternoon.

There's no one at the taxi stand,
no taxi, no passenger.

At the end of the street
a woman and a man embrace.

2

Early falling nights
grip the houses and let go.

Unlatching
the gate to his yard,

a boy's posture resembles
the posture of his father,

shoulders slumped, head down.
The clouds he doesn't see

are brighter than
the moon he doesn't see.

3

Father gave me
the sadness of his childhood.

Mother, her stubbornness
and scrubby hair.

I want to grab her arm

and tell her I see
a weed at the edge of my yard

growing with such force

that by August its leafy stalk
towers over everything

and the pale blue flowers bloom,

wild, overlooked.

4

A church stands by a synagogue,

a widow in black
passes a teenager in black,

the brightness of glass balconies
dazes the cobblestones

as blue pigeons rise.

A woman and a man
resume the same argument,

it doesn't have an end.

A half-built apartment block
waits another year

for someone to work on it

or wonder at the windblown
patience of its rooms.

5

What will I give my son?

Which anger, which brightness

will tuck him in at night
in another year, will he

see through to the carpentry
in the stories I read him—

the poor miller's son
triumphs with his clever cat
and the barren fields revive—

or will he listen to the wolf
of his own imaginings

that turn him
inward on himself
in his dark moments, how

will I keep him safe,
which story, which hero—

6

In the day's margins, at the end

of summer, the slow

changes overtake
a woman and a man.

Whatever love they've made

is as uncertain
as the weeds' laughter

in the wind's dry throat.

In the House of a Friend of a Friend

Ten hours straight of falling snow.
The wires are down.

I'm tired of reading,
of getting up to check
the drift across the porch.

The log in the fireplace
takes a cue
from the lit newspaper,
it sprouts a yellow thorn.

Jeremiah knew
that loneliness is prophecy.
He foresaw the ruin
we are and have been.

This Morning

Forsythia, out of its mind—
        rolls of barbed wire in bloom.

Leaves come flooding
        to the trees, the light

dazed, amnesiac,
        like the sleeping-sickness

patient who forgot
        to age, her face smooth.

Sparrows dig through the shadowy
        cave of a hedge.

I'm driving, on the radio
        a man describes his first

seder in Munich
        after the camps closed,

how the few who gathered,
        friends of his, in their twenties,

asked the four questions—
    there were no children.

The man's voice breaks,
    he must be eighty or more...

No one told me
    the questions, growing up,

as if I couldn't be
    trusted with them.

Jazz now on the radio,
    the light the drifting light

that lets nothing go
    and holds nothing back,

the day, a wound
    I can't stop opening.

A crabapple branch
    sends its petals to the lawn.

Reading in Bed at the Inn

Rain falls on the streets
of gray Lisbon, Chapter 10.
The hero is letting himself

go, a day at a time,
unshaven, unshowered,
a sheaf of papers on the floor.

His coming death, hinted at
by his visions of Pessoa
writing a last poem

matters to me, its ache.
Now evening and snow—the sky's
only decision all day,

sifting through the trees.
What if this night buries me
under the bedspread, by the lamp?

Fourth Room of the Exhibition

After the portraits in three rooms,
the women, prisoners
      of heavy velvet sleeves
            and the keys at their waists,

the men, of their own deliberateness,
their hounds and set lips,
      this other painting, by the door:
            the back of a man who steps

naked through a parted drape
into a room so dark I can't
      penetrate its function or his need.
            He has your build—

sturdy back, strong legs,
generous buttocks that know
      long work and nights of love.
           His haunches are carved to hold

the weight of his heat and bitterness
and the weight of one
      he comes to in the dark
           in a room that enters him.

Longing in Passover Week

I've heard
the strange sounds
of the prayers

but only the way a mule,
deaf to its own name,
looks up
from a mouthful of hay.

.   .

*La Pascua
de los Judíos*—

the holiday
of Jews—

a label
on a box

of candies
in a store

in the north
of Spain,

a curiosity.

.   .

Myrtle and fig
by the road
that year.

Sometimes
we collapsed
on the sagging mattress
in the middle
of our room
in the middle of the day,

the wind's
translation of the trees
knotting us together before rain.

.   .

*Who can hear
how all trees sing to God—*

in the book
I read again last night.

This morning,
the mourning dove

repeats the same thing.

Summer as a Large, Reclining Nude

These are the days when summer lies
naked on the lawn, indolent and hot,
careless of the sparrows on her limbs.
She yawns deep within the pleasure of her mass,
giant breasts, belly, thighs, and knees,
pockets of moisture soaking in the sun.
Across the street, a radio drones on,
describing the rank and file of two armies
dragging their equipment to the line
though a war seems far-fetched this late
in August. We're sleeping in the fear
of infinitely heavy arms and legs,
weeks defying the measurements of Thoth.
The rose nude yawns, rolls over in the grass,
draws us closer with a gorgeous laugh.

Drifting

Córdoba, under a layer of clouds.
The tall stalks of the poplars,
each round leaf glittering.

I've already died
and this is my resting place.
The afternoon is huge.

Córdoba, in hard bright light.
Past the scattered orange trees
with their sour fruit,

a fountain, a stone bench.
Ghosts streaming out of the gates
that lead to the white nest

of the *judería*'s tangled streets.
A skein of eyes. A knot of flies.
Little by little, day is slain.

I breathe in slow. I sip
at a small table in the dark.
I'm looking around the square

for something I can memorize.
A statue, a thick cross.
A pointed star, a door.

Pines

The wind behind
our peeling house
ties itself to the pines
and they set sail.

We doze and wake
fitfully, like those
who never truly hold
or put a thing away.

When Hamlet said,
*What a piece of work
is man,* he must have meant
the marvel of the hand

that poisons, and caresses,
finds the folds
of a woman's pleasure,
unbuttons a man.

Hand that holds
a knife. That lays it down.

Travels in Place

Which is in my blood,
the snows of Lithuania
or the dark sunshine of Navarre?

Which is it, the wind
tantrumming through Galicia
or the dry heat of Jerusalem?

Or neither, neither,
maybe my blood only knows
the airless New England summer

falling to winter again—
snow and rain, and cold blue days
in stiff Puritanical clothes.

Instead of the cedars of Lebanon,
the dogwood, waiting for spring.
Oak, maple, beech.

Blue spruce and white pine.
Maybe blood is a fiction.
Maybe I only know

the snow that falls
without a beginning or end
from every window of the house.

Reading Borges While the Baby Naps

My living room, a library,
the afternoon, a labyrinth
where faces disappear
like rain in a river.

Under the bones of my hand,
pages are shadows.
A soldier, Borges' ancestor,
listens for enemy fire.

Blue air, blown grass,
the bullet he foresaw.
Almost awake, the baby
dreams of being awake

and trembles, waits to be floated
out of sleep, into time
which lifts the dust
in its hem above the floor.

Blue Dress

I slept and slept
as if Caliban had rolled
the boulder of his body onto mine

and I could breathe,
breath but not move.

I couldn't shake the stupor off.

Weeks floated like drowned bees.

If there had been a shipwreck,
if I was missing something
beneath the waves,

I didn't want to look.

.   .

The dress I bought
       for larger months,
blue dress with feathery
          white flowers on green stems,

    two pockets in the front:
 I'm emptied, empty

imagining loose petals
  on unwinding stems
now that I have bled,
  now that spring and summer
    won't make any difference.

Summer has grown old,
  a loose dress, hiding nothing.

Table

Give me oysters, the purple and green
puddle in each shell, their rough white rims,
the plate where they gather, skiffs
on a pond. Everything simple: the stocky
reassuring knife, the lavender pitcher,
lemons blazing beneath their skins
on a blue mat, the blue mat on a larger
square of pink bordered with red,
red to the limits of the field
of vision: this is the feast I need.

The Adoption

October leapt out
with a barrel-chested laugh.

A gust of wind
unhinged the sparrows

from the maple.
The baby, too, laughed deep

as though being here
were nothing she had planned

but she got the joke,
the lovely, lovely joke.

Judía

In Spain: the green bean—
long, crooked, and curved.

The word for Jew, feminine.
A green bean, a feature, a nose.

A garden, stripped to singleness,
remnant the wind frayed.

The green beans I had there
were delicious and cheap.

I ate them with equally fresh
tomatoes, a warm loaf of bread.

Spain, I have more names
than a cherry tree has leaves.

Let me sleep with you tonight
half a world away,

forgetting the sad centuries.
Just you and me, and the warm spring night.

Notes

The trolley lurches past,
tying its stops together
with a string of sparks.

The spring air is blowing
plastic sheets on the scaffolding
into ripe sails. We

sit down on the steps
of the temple with its Moorish dome,
the doors, wooden pages.

The small dark notes
of the night begin
like so many sparrows

scattering before us in
a sparrow diaspora,
choosing this time to call their own.

Notes

I am indebted to James Carroll's *Constantine's Sword: The Church and the Jews,* New York: Houghton Mifflin Co., 2001, *Guía Judía de España,* edited by Juan G. Atienza, Madrid: Altalena Editores, S.A., 1978, and *Jews, Christians, and Muslims in the Mediterranean World After 1492,* edited by Alisa Meyuhas Ginio, London: Frank Cass and Company, Ltd., 1992.

"Conspiracy of Silence." Amrita Pritam is the author of more than fifty books in Punjabi and Urdu, including poetry, novels, short stories, and memoirs. Her work has been translated into many languages.

"Hymns in the Wind" is in memory of André Favat, teacher.

"*from* The Word." Irfan Malik is a poet and short-story writer who grew up in Lahore and now lives in the States. His second volume of poetry, *Untold,* was published in both Pakistan and India.

"A *Judeo-converso,* ca. 1470": The phrase "*Adonai, adóname*"—the latter word a conflation of Adonai and the Spanish verb *donar* (to grant, bestow), was reported in an Inquisition document relating to Francisco de Montealegre, of Cuenca, Spain, who died of illness circa 1470. This information appears in "Nostalgia for the Past (and for the Future?) among Castilian Judeoconversos" by Carlos Carrete

Parrondo, in *Jews, Christians, and Muslims in the Mediterranean World After 1492*.

"Leaving" and "1497": Excerpts from R. Abraham Saba's painful account of himself and his family during the expulsions of the Jews first from Spain and then Portugal appear in "Autobiographical Elements in the Writings of Kabbalists from the Generation of the Expulsion" by Michael Oron, in *Jews, Christians, and Muslims in the Mediterranean World After 1492*.

"Song." Najam Hussain Syed is the most influential writer in the rediscovery of Punjabi as a literary language. He is the author of several volumes of poetry, in addition to plays and criticism.

"Longing in Passover Week": the book referred to in part 3 of the poem is Abraham Joshua Heschel's *Man's Quest for God*, in which he asks, "Whose ear has ever heard how all trees sing to God?"

JENNIFER BARBER grew up in Massachusetts, attended Colby College in Maine, and studied medieval literature in England as a Rhodes Scholar. She received her MFA from Columbia University. A selection of her work appears in the anthology *Take Three: 3, Agni New Poets Series* (Graywolf Press, 1998); a selection also appears in the anthology *Four Way Reader #2* (Four Way Books, 2001).

She is founding and current editor of the literary journal *Salamander*, and has taught at Wellesley College, Bradford College, and the Harvard Extension School. She has lived in England, Canada, New York City, and Spain, and now lives with her husband and two children in Brookline, Mass. She received a Bruce P. Rossley New Voices Award in 1998.